W9-CIC-037

Your Government:
How It Works

The Cabinet

Sam Wellman

Arthur M. Schlesinger, jr.
Senior Consulting Editor

Chelsea House Publishers
Philadelphia

CHELSEA HOUSE PUBLISHERS

Production Manager Pamela Loos
Art Director Sara Davis
Director of Photography Judy L. Hasday
Managing Editor James D. Gallagher
Senior Production Editor J. Christopher Higgins

Staff for THE CABINET

Project Editor/Publishing Coordinator Jim McAvoy
Associate Art Director Takeshi Takahashi
Series Designers Takeshi Takahashi, Keith Trego

The Chelsea House World Wide Web address is
http://www.chelseahouse.com

First Printing
1 3 5 7 9 8 6 4 2

Library of Congress Cataloging-in-Publication Data

Wellman, Sam.
      The Cabinet / Sam Wellman.
          p. cm.—(Your government—how it works)
      Includes bibliographical references and index.
      ISBN 0-7910-5993-6
          1. Cabinet Officers—United States—Juvenile literature.
      2. Executive departments—United States—Juvenile literature.
      [1. Cabinet Officers. 2. Executive departments 3. United States—
      Politics and government.] I. Title. II. Series.

      JK611 .W45 2000
      352.24'0973—dc21   00-034576

Contents

YOUR GOVERNMENT
HOW IT WORKS

Introduction

Government: Crises of Confidence

Arthur M. Schlesinger, jr.

FROM THE START, Americans have regarded their government with a mixture of reliance and mistrust. The men who founded the republic understood the importance of government. "If men were angels," observed the 51st Federalist Paper, "no government would be necessary." But men are not angels. Because human beings are subject to wicked as well as to noble impulses, government was deemed essential to assure freedom and order.

The American revolutionaries, however, also knew that government could become a source of injury and oppression. The men who gathered in Philadelphia in 1787 to write the Constitution therefore had two purposes in mind: They wanted to establish a strong central authority and to limit that central authority's capacity to abuse its power.

To prevent the abuse of power, the Founding Fathers wrote two basic principles into the Constitution. The principle of federalism divided power between the state governments and the central authority. The principle of the separation of powers subdivided the central authority itself into three branches—the executive, the legislative, and the judiciary—so that "each may be a check on the other."

YOUR GOVERNMENT: HOW IT WORKS examines some of the major parts of that central authority, the federal government. It explains how various officials, agencies, and departments operate and explores the political organizations that have grown up to serve the needs of government.

Introduction

The federal government as presented in the Constitution was more an idealistic construct than a practical administrative structure. It was barely functional when it came into being.

This was especially true of the executive branch. The Constitution did not describe the executive branch in any detail. After vesting executive power in the president, it assumed the existence of "executive departments" without specifying what these departments should be. Congress began defining their functions in 1789 by creating the Departments of State, Treasury, and War.

President Washington, assisted by Secretary of the Treasury Alexander Hamilton, equipped the infant republic with a working administrative structure. Congress also continued that process by creating more executive departments as they were needed.

Throughout the 19th century, the number of federal government workers increased at a consistently faster rate than did the population. Increasing concerns about the politicization of public service led to efforts—bitterly opposed by politicians—to reform it in the latter part of the century.

The 20th century saw considerable expansion of the federal establishment. More importantly, it saw growing impatience with bureaucracy in society as a whole.

The Great Depression during the 1930s confronted the nation with its greatest crisis since the Civil War. Under Franklin Roosevelt, the New Deal reshaped the federal government, assigning it a variety of new responsibilities and greatly expanding its regulatory functions. By 1940, the number of federal workers passed the 1 million mark.

Critics complained of big government and bureaucracy. Business owners resented federal regulation. Conservatives worried about the impact of paternalistic government on self-reliance, on community responsibility, and on economic and personal freedom.

When the United States entered World War II in 1941, government agencies focused their energies on supporting the war effort. By the end of World War II, federal civilian employment had risen to 3.8 million. With peace, the federal establishment declined to around 2 million in 1950. Then growth resumed, reaching 2.8 million by the 1980s.

A large part of this growth was the result of the national government assuming new functions such as: affirmative action in civil rights, environmental protection, and safety and health in the workplace.

Some critics became convinced that the national government was a steadily growing behemoth swallowing up the liberties of the people. The 1980s brought new intensity to the debate about government growth. Foes of Washington bureaucrats preferred local government, feeling it more responsive to popular needs.

But local government is characteristically the government of the locally powerful. Historically, the locally powerless have often won their human and constitutional rights by appealing to the national government. The national government has defended racial justice against local bigotry, upheld the Bill of Rights against local vigilantism, and protected natural resources from local greed. It has civilized industry and secured the rights of labor organizations. Had the states' rights creed prevailed, perhaps slavery would still exist in the United States.

Americans are still of two minds. When pollsters ask large, spacious questions—Do you think government has become too involved in your lives? Do you think government should stop regulating business?—a sizable majority opposes big government. But when asked specific questions about the practical work of government—Do you favor Social Security? Unemployment compensation? Medicare? Health and safety standards in factories? Environmental protection?—a sizable majority approves of intervention.

We do not like bureaucracy, but we cannot live without it. We need its genius for organizing the intricate details of our daily lives. Without bureaucracy, modern society would collapse. It would be impossible to run any of the large public and private organizations we depend on without bureaucracy's division of labor and hierarchy of authority. The challenge is to keep these necessary structures of our civilization flexible, efficient, and capable of innovation.

More than 200 years after the drafting of the Constitution, Americans still rely on government but also mistrust it. These attitudes continue to serve us well. What we mistrust, we are more likely to monitor. And government needs our constant attention if it is to avoid inefficiency, incompetence, and arbitrariness. Without our informed participation, it cannot serve us individually or help us as a people to attain the lofty goals of the Founding Fathers.

Abraham Lincoln, before announcing his decision to abolish slavery, discussed the issue with his cabinet. Most presidents have used the combined knowledge and experience of their cabinet members as a tool to help guide their decisions.

CHAPTER 1

What Does "Cabinet" Mean?

". . . THE SUBJECT IS ON my mind, by day and night, more than any other."

The subject was slavery. The speaker was Abraham Lincoln when he was president of the United States. The year was 1862. The United States had split into two parts over slavery. The Northern states wanted to free slaves. The Southern states wanted to keep slaves. Now the North and the South were fighting each other in the Civil War. As leader of the Northern states, Lincoln wanted to declare, or proclaim, all slaves free, or emancipated, including those in the Southern states. He intended to call this declaration the Emancipation Proclamation. Lincoln was sure that proclaiming all slaves free was the right thing to do.

But he still asked his cabinet for advice.

As head of the entire **executive branch** of government, President Lincoln met with his cabinet in his residence, the White House. His cabinet was a group that consisted of the top official from each of the seven departments of the executive branch. These seven were his main advisors. It didn't matter to Lincoln if a problem involved just one department or all seven. He wanted the advice of all his top officials. On September 22, 1862, Lincoln opened the cabinet meeting, as he often did, with a funny story to relax the group. He once said the war was so terrible, that if he didn't laugh once in a while, he would cry all the time. But that day most of the seven did not laugh. The war had soured them beyond laughing. There was a real possibility in 1862 that the North could lose the Civil War.

So Lincoln read his proclamation. In order to free the slaves, the government would pay their owners for them. But in any event, as of January 1, 1863, all slaves "shall be then, thence-forward, and forever free." He also proclaimed that the government would "recognize the freedom of such persons." Lincoln waited for advice from his cabinet.

Secretary of State William Seward suggested adding the words "and maintain" after "recognize." Lincoln liked that idea. Attorney General Edward Bates of the Department of Justice had supported the idea of proclaiming freedom for the slaves earlier. Now he hesitated. Wasn't Lincoln making black Americans equal to white Americans? The answer to that was so obvious Lincoln didn't comment. Postmaster General Montgomery Blair said he favored the announcement, but he was afraid it would cause some of the border states to rebel and join the South. Lincoln replied that he could not let the border states dictate the direction of the nation. Secretary of the Navy Gideon Welles agreed with the proclamation, justifying it as a "military necessity." It would discourage the Southern rebels and encourage the slaves.

If Secretary of War Edward Stanton, Secretary of the Interior Caleb Smith, and Secretary of the Treasury Samuel Chase disapproved of the proclamation, they did not voice any serious objections in the meeting. Lincoln had expected more advice from his cabinet. They were so glum and hesitant he could not resist another story. Lincoln told them about a hired man who came hesitantly to the farmer he worked for. The hired man told the farmer one of his two oxen had dropped dead. The farmer rushed to the stable where he kept the oxen. Both oxen were dead.

"Why didn't you tell me at once that both oxen were dead?" cried the farmer.

The hired man replied, "Because I didn't want to hurt you by telling you too much at one time."

President Lincoln thought his cabinet felt that way too. Still, the majority of his hesitant cabinet supported his decision. What would Lincoln have done if a majority of the seven cabinet members had opposed his proclamation? Probably he would have only delayed announcing it. Just two days later, from the balcony of the White House, President Abraham Lincoln peered down at a crowd and read the Emancipation Proclamation. All slaves would be officially free as of January 1, 1863.

To most Americans the word "cabinet" means an enclosed place with shelves for storing dishes, clothing, or supplies of some kind. So how in the world did the word cabinet come to also mean the top officials who work for the president of the United States? The answer to that question is far back in history—more than 100 years before the birth of the United States.

King Charles II, who ruled Britain from 1660 to 1685, brought the concept of a cabinet into use in the English-speaking world. A group called the Privy Council was supposed to advise British kings and queens. But by the time Charles II became king, the Privy Council had grown so

King Charles II is credited with having coined the term "cabinet" when speaking of his closest advisors. The influence of English rule carried over to America, and our presidents have continued to use a cabinet to help guide the country.

James Madison was the United States' fourth president. He is thought to have been the first to call his top advisors a cabinet.

large and unruly, it was an uproar of arguing voices. So Charles II selected a few leading members on the Privy Council for weekly meetings. Although people in Britain spoke English, King Charles II—who had lived in France for eight years before gaining the British throne—dubbed his small, private group with the French word "cabinet." In French cabinet means a small, private room. Only after Charles II had worked out an issue to his satisfaction with his cabinet did he meet with the full Privy Council. Naturally the full Privy Council soon had little influence with Charles II and with later British kings and queens. The cabinet wielded the real influence.

The founders of the United States—while they were still colonists—were subjects of Britain's King George III. The American colonies had been subject to British kings for many years before that. So most colonists not only spoke English but were very familiar with British law and customs. Even though the founders were determined enough to fight the Revolutionary War against Britain to be free of kings, they were still influenced by British customs. It was no surprise that in 1793 James Madison, who would some day become America's fourth president, began using the word cabinet for the top few officials in the president's executive branch of government. Madison also meant by the use of the word cabinet that meetings between the president of the United States and these officials were private. It would not be until 1907 that a law officially recognized a president's group of top advisors by the word cabinet.

The **Constitution,** the document that established the foundation for all law in the United States, spelled out the duties of the president and the executive branch. The Constitution assumed the president would carry out those duties by consulting with key advisors. Article II of the Constitution reads in part:

> The President . . . may require the Opinion, in writing, of the principal Officer in each of the executive Departments, upon any Subject relating to the Duties of their respective Offices . . .

And what were these executive departments? In New York City in 1789 Congress—the lawmaking, or legislative, branch of government—passed laws that officially established the executive branch: the Departments of Foreign Affairs, Treasury, and War. These were the same departments that had existed under the Articles of Confederation for the Continental Congress during the Revolutionary War. But within weeks Congress renamed the Department of Foreign Affairs. The principal duty of the head of that department was to conduct the foreign policy of the president of the United States. But Congress also assigned the head of that department duties that were domestic, that is, duties that were within the country. So Congress changed the name of the Department of Foreign Affairs to the Department of State.

CHAPTER 2

George Washington's Cabinet

THE INFANT UNITED STATES was very poor in 1789. Its first president, 57-year-old George Washington, had to borrow money to move from his Mount Vernon home in Virginia to the nation's capital, at that time in New York. When he arrived in New York the entire national government consisted of 75 post offices, 672 soldiers, and a large debt. The navy had disbanded. There was as yet no federal court system and no way to collect taxes.

Washington was humble, writing to a friend that he faced "an ocean of difficulties, without the competency of political skill, abilities, and inclinations which is necessary to manage the Chelm."

One of the founders, Gouveneur Morris, calmed him. "Your cool, steady temper is *indispensably necessary . . .* "

So Washington began his duties as president of the United States in much the same way he had begun his duties as the top American military commander during the Revolutionary War. He may not have been the most brilliant person in the young nation, but he was the most rock-solid, enduring, and inspiring. Only Ben Franklin was as much admired, but at 83, Franklin was of declining health. Americans thought the nation would persevere no matter how difficult things became—if Washington was in charge.

Although he was sworn in as president in April 1789, his three executive departments—Foreign Affairs, Treasury, and War—were not created by Congress until September. Throughout American history executive departments would be officially created by Congress, although often at the urging of the president. So it was not until September 1789 that Washington could select the principal officer in each of the executive departments. These principal officers would constitute his first cabinet. But President Washington did not call this select group of officials a "cabinet." "The heads of the great departments," some called the group.

James Madison, eventually the fourth president, began using the word cabinet in 1793. Whatever Washington first called his small group of powerful officials, he picked four brilliant men. The definition of the departments in the law passed by Congress was sketchy. The first heads had to design their own great departments.

Most people thought the Department of Foreign Affairs (renamed the Department of State, as mentioned earlier) was the most important executive department at this time in America's history. It was this department that would represent America to foreign powers. This department would negotiate treaties with other countries. When Washington became president, the foreign powers that most concerned him were England, France, and Spain. They were still well established in territories around the United States. Washington also wanted good relations with the many Native Americans. However, Congress—perhaps revealing its intentions—had assigned American Indian affairs to the Department of War.

Thomas Jefferson served as Washington's first secretary of state. He often disagreed with Washington and later resigned from the post.

In addition to its other duties, the Department of State was also supposed to safeguard the Great Seal, publish the Acts of Congress, draw up and record presidential commissions, file all applications for federal jobs, preserve the National Archives, receive copies of all copyrighted material, supervise territorial affairs, issue patents for inventions, and operate the federal mint.

"My chief comfort will be to work under your eye," was the way Washington's pick for secretary of state, Thomas Jefferson, answered him by letter.

At 46 Jefferson was well known in America. In 1776, at only 33, he had drafted the Declaration of Independence as a member of the Continental Congress. He had expressed the very essence of why the colonists wanted their freedom. There were few, if any, Americans who did not appreciate his eloquence. During most of the Revolutionary War Jefferson had been governor of Virginia. But in 1782 he went as America's diplomat to France, a country that proved to be a powerful ally against England. So Jefferson already had much experience dealing with foreign powers.

For the Department of the Treasury Washington wanted Robert Morris. Washington had great respect for him. From 1781 to 1784 Morris had been a genius at financing the Revolutionary War, often using his own personal credit. In Philadelphia he had established the Bank of North America, the oldest **financial** institution in the United States. But Robert Morris refused Washington.

The new president then asked 34-year-old Alexander Hamilton, his former aide in his military campaigns. The fiery Hamilton had already angered Washington a number of times, but the new president wanted the best official available. Hamilton was a phenomenon. He had been orphaned at the age of 13 in the West Indies. Yet somehow as a youth he had impressed bankers there with his aptitude for finance. He was sent to school in the American colonies, and he rose to political power in New York. He was every bit as brilliant as Jefferson. Besides managing the Postal Service, the secretary of the Treasury was charged with collecting taxes, issuing paper currency, and creating a banking system. "Extricate my country [from its debt]," Washington urged Hamilton.

For secretary of war, Washington selected his old artillery commander, Brigadier General Henry Knox, a 39-year-old Bostonian. He was a fighter from the very beginning of the Revolutionary War, having been one of the minutemen at Bunker Hill. He had fought in the battles of Princeton, Monmouth, and Yorktown. Washington felt very comfortable with Knox. But the truth was that the great Continental army of 60,000 had scattered to the four winds. Knox barely had one percent of that number in his standing army.

Least important in Washington's opinion was the office of **attorney general.** That official did not yet head a department. At that time the attorney general was understood to be the personal lawyer to the president. For the office Washington picked Edmund Randolph, a fellow Virginian and another former aide in his military campaigns. Randolph was no lightweight, having been governor of Virginia.

"I feel myself supported by able [officers]," Washington concluded, after selecting the heads of his departments.

It is certain that the president did not meet with his full cabinet until at least March 1790, when Thomas Jefferson returned to America from France. But it is not certain they ever met in the house Washington rented near Broadway and Wall Street in the first federal capital, New York City. Some historians believe Washington did not start meeting with the four until 1791. By that time the capital was in Philadelphia, where they met at the president's home on High (now Market) Street. And it was probably not until 1793 that Washington's cabinet met weekly.

During the birth of the nation Washington might well have given substantial duties to his vice president. Both Washington and his vice president had been elected by the electoral college, representatives of the 13 states. The general opinion in the electoral college was that if a "southerner" like Washington was president he had to be balanced by a "northerner" as vice president. So the electoral college had picked the very able but contrary John Adams of Massachusetts. Washington was uncomfortable with Adams, a blunt man who had often criticized him. So Washington ignored Adams, and Adams did not participate in Washington's cabinet. If John Adams had been agreeable to Washington, history might have been very different for vice presidents. Some historians think that the vice president might have become like England's prime minister, one of the most powerful officials in the nation. But that was not to be.

". . . (Washington) wisely used the qualities of able men while ignoring their faults," observed one historian. But that applied only to people Washington had picked, not John Adams. Even in Washington's tiny cabinet of four there was friction at times. The two most powerful members, Hamilton and Jefferson, constantly rubbed each other the wrong way. Some said they were "born to hate each other." Except for both of them being smart and accomplished, they differed in every other way. Hamilton rose from poverty. Jefferson was aristocratic. Hamilton was short and wiry, while Jefferson was tall and slouchy. Hamilton dressed as a dandy. Jefferson often dressed sloppily. Hamilton was aggressive. Jefferson was polite.

But there was a much more important source of tension between them. They represented the two dominant political philosophies of the time. Hamilton was a "federalist," one who wanted a very strong federal government. Jefferson was a "republican," but this did not mean then what it meant later: a member of a political party. In Jefferson's day a **republic** was a nation made up of individual states, so a republican was one who wanted to keep very strong state governments. A federalist like Hamilton envisioned America as a manufacturing and trading giant with a powerful central government. A republican like Jefferson envisioned America as a nation of prosperous farms with strong state governments.

Jefferson's 18th-century republicanism seems odd in the 21st century. How could he have envisioned the United States as a nation of high-minded farmers? But in his time it was not odd at all. Nineteen of every 20 Americans lived on farms or in small villages. It should not be thought that Jefferson desired a country of gentleman farmers like the privileged aristocrats of Britain. To the contrary, he stated clearly that by whatever reforms necessary he wanted "a system by which every fibre would be eradicated of ancient or future aristocracy; and a foundation laid for a government truly republican . . . "

Over the first few years of Washington's **presidency** Jefferson's dream of a perfect farming society slowly evaporated. Hamilton seemed to prevail on every issue. He established a federal bank, which alarmed all the republicans. Yet it was just one more sign that the new nation was getting a strong **federal** government. The final proof was the decision to build a national capital—named Washington, D.C.—from the ground up. Yet Jefferson found he had to suggest designs, because the city could be "offensive to the eye, if not well managed."

During the 18th century the majority of Americans worked on farms. Thomas Jefferson had hoped that the United States would become a nation of farmers governed by each individual state.

By 1793 Jefferson had almost despaired of this trend to federalism under President Washington. But the final blow came when Hamilton began interfering with Jefferson's foreign policy. Jefferson would not tolerate that. Feeling that Washington was not supporting him, Jefferson resigned from Washington's cabinet. Attorney General Randolph, who had distinguished himself mainly by staying neutral in the feud between Hamilton and Jefferson, replaced Jefferson as secretary of state.

Alexander Hamilton was a federalist who envisioned the United States as an industrial giant with a strong centralized government. Disagreements between Hamilton and Jefferson would eventually end with both leaving their positions in Washington's cabinet.

By 1795 Randolph also resigned his position. A message sent to him from France hinted that he may have accepted a bribe. Whether or not it was true, he left Washington's cabinet, very angry that Washington was unwilling to dismiss the hint. Ironically, Hamilton left the cabinet that year too. Though he had stirred up much trouble for others, he had been attacked often, too. Hamilton no longer wanted the intense criticism. Henry Knox had already resigned in 1794 to attend his neglected personal business, which was a mess. So in 1795—six years since the beginning of Washington's cabinet—all the original members were gone. "[Attacks on me have] shaken a determination which I thought the whole world could not have shaken," Jefferson had said when he resigned his post.

By 1795 Thomas Pickering from Massachusetts was secretary of state. Secretary of the Treasury was Oliver Wolcott from Connecticut. Secretary of war was Maryland's James McHenry, another former military aide to Washington. All three men were not only federalists but strong admirers of Hamilton. The new attorney general, Charles Lee, had little influence. Clearly, Washington's main advisors continued the thrust toward a strong, centralized federal government.

Were Washington's new cabinet members as competent as their predecessors? Most historians don't think so. First of all, the resignation of Jefferson had made most of his fellow republicans unwilling to serve in a cabinet dominated by federalists. Secondly, even federalists were reluctant to serve. Being a member of the cabinet brought intense scrutiny and abusive criticism. President Washington tended to stand off at the side and let matters take their course. Why did he do that? Because he was very aware that he was so popular—already legendary for his many heroics—that he could win on almost any issue. And he had no wish to be a tyrant like a king. So the most able people now refused to serve him.

Yet many ambitious people waited for the next presidency.

Cautioned by wars in Europe, President John Adams made the first addition to the cabinet by creating the secretary of the navy.

CHAPTER **3**

Two Hundred Years of Growth and Change

IN 1796, JOHN ADAMS, after being ignored for eight years as vice president, ran against Thomas Jefferson for president. By then the two political philosophies—federalism and republicanism—about what direction America should take had become real political parties. Washington didn't like "spirit of party" because he thought it caused people to prefer the good of their political party to the good of the nation. But political parties had become a reality. Adams ran as a Federalist, the party that wanted a strong federal government and favored industry, landowners, and merchants. Jefferson ran as a Democratic-Republican, the party that emphasized personal liberty and limited powers for the federal government. Adams narrowly defeated Jefferson. Yet the two men respected each other's abilities.

Nevertheless, Jefferson let Adams know that he wanted no cabinet position. "I cannot have a wish to . . . [again] descend daily into the arena like a gladiator."

President Adams blundered by keeping Washington's cabinet. Yes, that cabinet supported Adams's federalism but, with the exception of Charles Lee, was loyal to Alexander Hamilton. Pickering, Wolcott, and McHenry constantly consulted Hamilton rather than Adams. Partly because of this Adams's presidency rocked from crisis to crisis. Yet Adams is significant in the history of the cabinet. He was the first president to host his cabinet at the newly finished White House. Next to his office was a large room for his library and the cabinet meeting. This room was later expanded into the State Dining Room.

It was during the Adams presidency that construction started next to the White House on the first separate buildings for the executive departments. In addition Adams increased the number of cabinet members to five by adding a secretary of the navy in 1798. His new secretary of the navy, Benjamin Stoddert, began building a fleet of warships. Adams ordered this because France, led by Napoleon, was provoking battles with many countries. "[The French] respected the new United States Navy," noted one historian.

Adams was succeeded by Thomas Jefferson in 1801. Did this visionary change the nature of the cabinet? No. Nor did his successors James Madison, James Monroe, and John Quincy Adams. But the same could not be said for Andrew Jackson, America's hot-tempered seventh president in the years 1829 to 1837. Jackson—like Washington—was a national hero. He had won his fame in the War of 1812 against the British. First of all, Jackson made it plain he wanted no cabinet officer who accepted the position as a political stepping-stone. Too often in the past, Jackson thought, political ambition by a cabinet member had led to decisions that were contrary to what the president wanted. Jackson noted that Monroe, Madison, Jefferson, and John Quincy Adams had all first been cabinet officers. But Jackson himself was very political. He took the Postal Service away from the Department of the Treasury. He made the postmaster general—in this case his old political friend William T. Barry—a cabinet member. Through Barry, Jackson began the practice of awarding hundreds of post office jobs to political friends. "To the victor belongs the spoils," growled Jackson's defenders.

This custom of using the post office to award loyal party workers would continue for 131 years—until 1970 (as we'll see later on). Jackson's cynical use of the cabinet was revealed another way. For two of his eight years as president he refused to meet with his cabinet members. Instead he sought advice from his political friends, who came to be known as his "Kitchen Cabinet." On the other hand, Jackson's mandate that cabinet positions not be used as a stepping-stone for higher office was worthless. His own secretary of state, Martin Van Buren, succeeded him as president in 1837.

Jackson was a hard act to follow. No significant changes were made in the operation of the cabinet until 1849. Because America was constantly adding new lands, during President James Polk's presidency Congress established the Department of the Interior. This department was to supervise the use of government land, administer American Indian affairs, and take a national census every 10 years— as well as issue patents on inventions. Polk, however, did not appoint the first secretary of the new department. President Zachary Taylor had that privilege in 1849, appointing Thomas Ewing of Ohio as secretary of the interior.

In 1870 President Ulysses Grant was able to put the attorney general in charge of an official Justice Department. No further changes in the cabinet occurred until Grover Cleveland's presidency in 1889. Although Abraham Lincoln had established a Department of Agriculture in 1862, its head did not get cabinet rank. Cleveland changed that, elevating Norman J. Colman of Missouri to secretary of agriculture. Colman had helped his own cause by being innovative as Cleveland's commissioner of agriculture. He was key in authoring the Hatch Act of 1887,

Natural wonders, such as Old Faithful, are often protected by our government. The supervision of government lands falls under the responsibilities of the secretary of the interior. The first secretary of the interior was appointed in 1849.

which helped bring about the program for agricultural experiment stations. Colman's new cabinet job was to inform the president of farmers' concerns as well as to dispense information about modern farming techniques. Cleveland met with his eight cabinet members in the Treaty Room on the second floor of the White House.

"[There must be an] increase in governmental power over big business," said Theodore Roosevelt, America's 26th president.

It was no surprise, then, that in 1903 he established a new cabinet position: secretary of **commerce** and **labor.** Since 1884 the Department of the Interior had monitored workers with its Bureau of Labor. But by 1903 business was booming. America was an industrial giant. Both business and labor needed attention. This ninth member of the cabinet—the secretary of commerce and labor—was to monitor all business and labor activities. The first secretary was George B. Cortelyou from New York. Both business interests and labor interests, although usually at odds, were supposed to be represented fairly. Roosevelt made another notable change. He and his cabinet met in an official "cabinet room" in the White House.

In the 19th and early 20th centuries it was not uncommon for children to work long hours in places such as mines and factories. Child labor was one of many issues which were controlled by the secretary of labor, a position created in 1913.

By 1913 it was recognized that the secretary of commerce and labor could not represent two opposing views. So President Woodrow Wilson split the job into a secretary of commerce and a secretary of labor. The first full-time secretary of labor was William B. Wilson of Pennsylvania. One of his main duties was to watch for abuses in the business boom. Were workers subjected to hazards? Were workers laboring too many hours? Were they being paid fairly? Were children being worked too hard? The first full-time secretary of commerce was William C. Redfield. His duty was to promote American business, both at home and in foreign countries. The president's cabinet members now numbered 10.

"Many of the unofficial cabinet . . . brought to Washington [by President Franklin Roosevelt in 1933] were more important than the real cabinet," noted a historian years later. Perhaps that explains why Franklin Roosevelt, although he served as president nearly 13 years, added no cabinet positions. He did, though, appoint the first woman to a cabinet position. Frances Perkins, an accomplished **civil servant** and social reformer from New York, became secretary of labor in 1933. She served throughout Roosevelt's presidency. In terms of longevity, Harold Ickes, secretary of the interior, also served throughout Roosevelt's term, but continued on into Harry Truman's presidency too, totaling 14 years of service.

President Truman provides a good example of the old axiom, "Be careful what you ask for. You just might get it!" The army and air force were clamoring for their own cabinet posts, similar to the cabinet post for the navy. Truman realized it did seem awkward to have a secretary of war and a secretary of the navy and no secretaries of the army or air force. But in 1947 Truman eliminated the secretary of the navy as a cabinet position. The number of cabinet members dropped to nine. Truman combined the departments of war and navy into one Department of Defense. James V. Forrestal of New York, Truman's secretary

of the navy, became the first secretary of defense. Forrestal had been a major behind-the-scenes figure in World War II, directing a huge expansion of the navy. Truman gave Forrestal the duty of reorganizing the armed services after the war.

In 1953 President Dwight Eisenhower boosted the number of cabinet positions to 10 again by establishing the Department of Health, Education, and Welfare. The new department absorbed six older agencies not of cabinet rank: the Public Health Service, the Office of Education, the Food and Drug **Administration,** the National Institute of Health, the Social Security Administration, and the Welfare Administration. For this very important new department Eisenhower appointed Oveta Culp Hobby, the second woman to be a cabinet member. Hobby was a well-qualified executive. In World War II she had organized and directed the Women's Army Corps.

President Lyndon Johnson stressed an America "where every human being has dignity . . . and employment is unaware of race." Although in his six-year presidency Johnson

Secretary of the Navy James V. Forrestal fires a 240mm howitzer in Italy during World War II. President Harry S. Truman would later create the secretary of defense and appoint Forrestal as the first to hold the position.

Robert C. Weaver was appointed to President Lyndon Johnson's cabinet in 1965. Not only was Weaver the first African American to be appointed to the cabinet, he was also the first secretary of housing and urban development.

had no women in his cabinet, he did appoint the first African American, Robert C. Weaver of Washington, D.C., to a cabinet post in 1965. Weaver also became the first secretary of housing and urban development. The Harvard-educated Weaver was well experienced in both state and federal housing aspects. President Johnson wanted him to manage housing loans, construction, and slum clearance. Two years later Johnson established a second new department: Transportation. America needed coordination of its enormous expansion of ground and air traffic. Alan S. Boyd of Florida was the first secretary of transportation.

The number of cabinet posts actually dropped from 12 to 11 during Richard Nixon's presidency. The Postal Service was split off in 1970 as a separate corporation. Not only did Nixon eliminate postmaster general as a cabinet post, he ended the long tradition of awarding post office jobs to political party workers. Like some previous presidents, Nixon did not necessarily have his most powerful advisors in the cabinet. He constantly depended on National Security Advisor Henry Kissinger.

"Henry Kissinger had taken the office [of National Security Advisor] to the heights of power, eclipsing the State Department," wrote one former National Security Council member. "When he became Secretary of State, he held on to the NSC post for a while to make sure no one could do the same to him."

President Jimmy Carter restored the number of cabinet posts to 12 in 1977 by establishing the Department of Energy. Foreign countries were withholding the supply of oil, so Carter felt America had to better manage its own energy resources. The first secretary of energy was James

Schlesinger of Virginia. But Carter was not through. In 1979 he split the Department of Health, Education, and Welfare into a Department of Education and a Department of Health and Human Services. The first secretary of education was Shirley M. Hufstedler, a judge from California. The first secretary of health and human services was Patricia R. Harris. In 1965 Harris had already distinguished herself as the first African-American woman to become an ambassador, serving in Luxembourg.

President Ronald Reagan inherited 13 cabinet posts and made no changes in eight years. Reagan did appoint the first Hispanic-American to a cabinet post. Lauro Fred Cavazos Jr., an educator from Texas, became secretary of education in 1988. Reagan also signed the law that would create a new cabinet post after he left office. It was President George Bush, who had been the youngest naval pilot in World War II, who appointed Edward J. Derwinski of Illinois as the first secretary of veteran affairs in 1989. Derwinski had been an infantryman in World War II. Affairs for veterans of military service were organized into seven main categories: health care and rehabilitation, education, insurance, counseling, pensions, home loans, and burial benefits.

President Bush, in a swearing-in ceremony for his new cabinet member, said simply, "There is only one place for the veterans of America, in the Cabinet Room, at the table with the President of the United States of America." Bush also noted that a quote from Abraham Lincoln at the front entrance of the Veterans Affairs Department stated its mission: "to care for him who shall have borne the battle and for his widow and his orphan."

No cabinet posts were added from 1989 to 2000. Now let us examine each of the 14 cabinet posts in their modern forms.

Secretary of State Madeleine Albright meets with United Nations Secretary-General Kofi Annan during the Kosovo conflict. The secretary of state has always been an integral member of the president's cabinet and faces numerous challenges as the country moves into the 21st century.

CHAPTER 4

The Original Cabinet Posts in the 21st Century

WHEN THE 21ST CENTURY arrived, the most powerful members of the president's cabinet remained those in the original four positions—official titles altered in some cases—that advised George Washington in the 18th century. Over the years, eight individuals who held one of these four cabinet posts later became presidents of the United States. But in 211 years, what happened specifically to the original four cabinet posts—the secretaries of state, Treasury, and war, plus the attorney general?

Secretary of State

The Department of State that first Secretary of State Thomas Jefferson operated with five clerks certainly changed. Over the years it shed itself of domestic chores like handling patents for inventions and operating the mint. Its primary responsibility became the president's foreign policy, just as the original name Department of Foreign Affairs indicated. Decisions on foreign policy made by past presidents were usually based on information provided by the State Department. Naturally, the conduct of foreign affairs has always aimed to protect the long-range interests and security of the United States.

Since 1947 the department has been housed about half a mile southwest of the White House in an area called Foggy Bottom. The Department of State did not become a huge department, compared to the other executive departments. In the year 2000 its 25,000 employees worked with an annual budget of about $5 billion. That was the smallest budget of all 14 departments. But that budget does not indicate the relative importance of the State Department or the secretary of state. Congress has always considered the secretary of state the most powerful department head in the president's cabinet.

Laws passed in 1947 and later years offer proof of the importance of the secretary of state to the nation. Congress established the "line of succession" to the presidency. After the vice president, Speaker of the House of Representatives and **president** *pro tempore* **of the Senate** comes the secretary of state. So law ranks the secretary of state the fourth most qualified individual to succeed the president. Also in 1947 the National Security Act established the National Security Council to assist the president on national security and foreign policy. By law one of the six council members must be the secretary of state.

Many secretaries of state became national figures. Thomas Jefferson, James Madison, James Monroe, John Quincy Adams, Martin Van Buren, and James Buchanan all went on to become presidents. Four secretaries of state won Nobel Peace Prizes: Frank Kellogg, Cordell Hull, George Marshall, and Henry Kissinger. Many others are famous historical figures: John Marshall, Daniel Webster,

Henry Clay, William Seward, William Jennings Bryan, Dean Acheson, and John Foster Dulles.

In the year 2000 this is how the Department of State described its own mission: "U.S. diplomacy is an instrument of power, essential for maintaining effective international relationships, and a principal means through which the United States defends its interests, responds to crises, and achieves its international goals. The Department of State is the lead institution for the conduct of American diplomacy, a mission based on the role of the Secretary of State as the President's principal foreign policy adviser."

In order to carry out foreign policy the secretary of state is served directly by one deputy secretary, a number of undersecretaries, a large headquarters staff, and many workers in foreign countries. The position of undersecretary of public diplomacy and public affairs was created in 1999. This official had a new major branch formed by combining the Arms Control and Disarmament Agency and the United States Information Agency. Other major branches of the Department of State are run by undersecretaries for management; global affairs; economic, business and agricultural affairs; and political affairs.

The undersecretary of political affairs and seven assistant secretaries run the enormous worldwide network of over 200 embassies and consulates. Normally every foreign country has an American embassy run by an American ambassador. Ambassadors are appointed by the president and confirmed by the Senate. This "diplomatic mission" is the primary contact with the U.S. government for nationals of that country as well as for Americans in that country. Many an American traveler has received help in a foreign country at the American embassy. Recently the State Department has also employed a "country-team" approach. Not just those in Political Affairs but workers from other branches deal with problems relating to a specific country.

Secretary of the Treasury

The Department of the Treasury, also established in 1789, began constructing its enormous Greek revival–style building immediately east of the White House in 1836. Of all the executive department buildings in 2000, it was the oldest. By the year 2000 the secretary of the Treasury directed an annual budget of $400 billion and 146,000 employees. The Department of the Treasury is organized into departmental offices and operating bureaus. Bureaus make up 98 percent of the Treasury workforce. The basic functions of the Department of the Treasury are carried out by its many bureaus (some of which do not carry the name "bureau").

★ The Bureau of Alcohol, Tobacco, and Firearms has two major functions. It is responsible for enforcing laws on the production, use, and distribution of alcohol and tobacco products. It also has the same responsibility with laws about guns and explosives.

★ The Office of the Comptroller of the Currency was established in 1863 to regulate the National Banking System. In 2000 about 2,300 bank examiners monitored banks.

★ The Internal Revenue Service (IRS) is charged with collecting many forms of taxes: personal income, corporate income, excise, estate, and gift taxes, as well as employment taxes for the Social Security system.

★ The United States Mint was created to mint the nation's coins. Also, the mint manages the famous Fort Knox that holds the federal government's entire reserve of gold.

★ The Bureau of Engraving and Printing makes paper currency, postage stamps, customs and revenue stamps, as well as Treasury bills and other U.S. securities.

★ The Financial Management Service receives and disburses all public monies, maintains government accounts, and prepares regular reports on government finances. The FMS disburses in excess of $1 trillion every year.

★ The Bureau of the Public Debt borrows money needed to operate the federal government. It accomplishes its mission by issuing and servicing marketable U.S. Treasury securities.

★ The United States Savings Bonds Division promotes the sale and retention of savings bonds.

★ The Secret Service became best known as the agency that protects the president. Yet it was established in 1865 for the purpose of stopping criminals from counterfeiting money. The Secret Service also protects the vice president, major candidates for offices, former presidents, and visiting foreign dignitaries.

★ The Customs Service enforces laws about imports and exports at U.S. ports of entry. This agency is the first line of defense in the nation's war on drugs.

★ The Office of Thrift Supervision regulates all savings institutions chartered by federal and state governments.

★ The Federal Law Enforcement Training Center instructs agents and officers from various governmental law enforcement agencies, even outside the Department of the Treasury.

★ The Financial Crimes Enforcement Network investigates international money laundering.

★ The Community Development Financial Institutions promote investment to develop communities.

The secretaries of the Treasury have been much less in the spotlight than the secretaries of state. Few became household names. Perhaps the best known remains the original: Alexander Hamilton. Hamilton, a federalist who campaigned tirelessly for a strong central government, had enormous influence in the founding of America. He seemed destined to become president, but he was killed in a duel at the age of 49.

Secretary of Defense

President Washington's tiny Department of War—with a mere 672 soldiers in 1789—grew to a gigantic organization by the year 2000. Its annual budget by that year was nearly $300 billion. Civilian workers numbered about 700,000. Military personnel numbered over 1,300,000. Headquarters for the department is just across the Potomac River from Washington, D.C., in the Pentagon.

That five-sided edifice is one of the largest buildings in the world. The Pentagon covers 30 acres. The distance from the center of the five-acre courtyard to the outermost wall is about 200 yards. It actually consists of five concentric pentagons around a central courtyard. By 2000 workers in the Pentagon numbered 23,000, so it also has a shopping center, a food-service area, bus and taxi terminals, and a port for helicopters. Often the Department of Defense itself is referred to as "the Pentagon."

The mission of the Department of Defense is to provide the military force needed to prevent war and to protect the security of America. Reporting to the Department of Defense through a chain of command are four armed services (the army, navy, air force, and marines) and 14 defense agencies. The military services recruit, train, and equip their forces. However, those forces are usually operated by one of nine "unified combatant commands." These commands, which are geographical (Atlantic, Pacific, European, etc.), combine all branches. Many other support agencies exist in the Department of Defense.

The secretary of defense, once known as the secretary of war, is rivaled in importance only by the secretary of state. James Monroe, Ulysses S. Grant, and William Taft went on to become presidents after holding the post. Abraham Lincoln's son Robert once served as secretary of war.

Henry Stimson served as secretary from 1911 to 1913, then returned 27 years later to serve from 1940 to 1945. In between he was secretary of state from 1929 to 1933. The most ironic fact of all is that Jefferson Davis, who led the rebels of the South in the Civil War, had previously been America's secretary of war.

The Pentagon is one of the most recognized American buildings in the world. It serves as the headquarters for the department of defense and is the point from which all of the United States' military activities originate.

Attorney General

The position of attorney general was also established in 1789. Of the original four cabinet members, perhaps the attorney general has seen the most change. The office was originally envisioned as personal legal counsel for the president. The attorney general eventually headed an enormous Department of Justice. The one-person operation in George Washington's cabinet with virtually no budget had grown to a department with 125,000 personnel spending an annual budget of $18 billion by 2000. Headquarters of the Justice Department is about one-half mile southeast of the White House on Pennsylvania Avenue. Nearby the headquarters building is an equally massive edifice housing the department's Federal Bureau of Investigation (FBI).

Agents of the Federal Bureau of Investigation fall under the supervision of the Department of Justice. Considered by many as one of the world's greatest crime fighting organizations, the FBI reports back to the attorney general, who then, as a member of the cabinet, informs the president of any concerns.

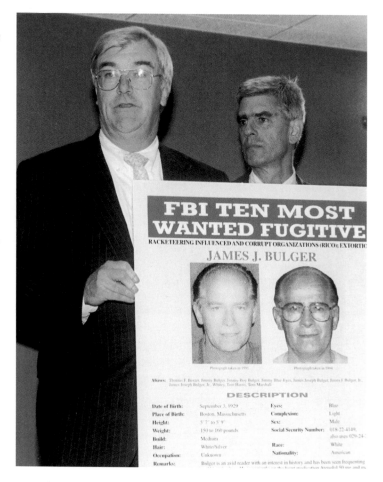

The department's mission is to provide leadership in preventing and controlling crime, as well as trying to ensure justice for all citizens. Regionally, each of 94 federal judicial districts has one U.S. attorney and one U.S. marshal. The attorney general's main helpers in Washington, D.C., are the deputy attorney general, the associate attorney general, and the solicitor general. Assistant attorneys general head several key divisions of the Department of Justice.

★ The Antitrust Division enforces federal antitrust laws.
★ The Civil Division supervises civil suits and claims involving the U.S. government. These include disputes over patents, copyrights, fraud, tort claims,

customs, immigration, international trade, veterans' affairs, and consumer affairs.

★ The **Civil Rights** Division is responsible for enforcing many civil rights laws passed since 1957. These laws mainly cover minorities and disabled persons.

★ The Criminal Division enforces laws relating to organized crime, kidnapping, bank robbery, fraud against the government, obscenity, corruption among public officials, drugs, racketeering, and national security.

★ The Environment and Natural Resources Division handles disputes involving public lands and natural resources, Native American lands and claims, wildlife resources, and environmental regulations.

★ The Tax Division pursues cases arising out of the internal revenue laws.

But the Department of Justice is even larger than that. Other agencies include the Federal Bureau of Investigation, which investigates violations of federal laws; the Bureau of Prisons; the U.S. Parole Commission; the Office of Justice Programs, which assists state and local law enforcement, supports research of justice issues, and compiles criminal justice statistics; the U.S. Marshals Service, which provides protection and other services for federal courts; the Drug Enforcement Administration; the Immigration and Naturalization Service; the Executive Office for Immigration Review; the Office of Special Counsel for Immigration-Related Unfair Employment Practices; the U.S. National Control Bureau–Interpol (international police); and the Foreign Claims Settlement Commission.

Attorneys general have rarely become well known. Not one has become president. The best-known attorney general was Robert Kennedy, who served under his brother, President John F. Kennedy, and President Lyndon Johnson. Janet Reno became the first female attorney general in 1993.

The Alaskan pipeline stretches across the tundra, delivering oil to the city of Valdez. Although natural resources, such as oil, fall under the supervision of the secretary of the interior, this particular resource will one day become the responsibility of the secretary of energy.

CHAPTER 5

The 10 Service-Resource Posts in the 21st Century

TEN CURRENT CABINET POSITIONS that were established after 1789 offer few famous people compared to the original four. Only one secretary has risen to president. President Herbert Hoover served as secretary of commerce. James Wilson was distinguished by serving 16 years as secretary of agriculture. George Cortelyou is unique in occupying three different cabinet posts under one president (Teddy Roosevelt). The 10 posts established after 1789 can be divided into two groups of five, one group heading departments that mainly serve individual citizens (Labor; Health and Human Services; Housing and Urban Development; Education; and Veterans Affairs) and one group heading departments that mainly shepherd national resources (Interior; Agriculture; Commerce; Transportation; and Energy).

Secretaries That Serve Individual Citizens

Secretary of Labor

The building housing the Department of Labor on Constitution Avenue is only one-quarter mile southeast of the White House. In the early 21st century the secretary of labor managed 38,000 employees with an annual budget of $16 billion. In 2000 the department declared its mission to be "preparing the American workforce for new and better jobs, and ensuring the adequacy of America's workplaces. [The department] is responsible for the administration and enforcement of over 180 federal statutes. These legislative mandates and the regulations produced to implement them cover a wide variety of workplace activities for nearly 10 million employers and well over 100 million workers, including protecting workers' wages, health and safety, employment and pension rights; promoting equal employment opportunity; administering job training, unemployment insurance and workers' compensation programs; strengthening free collective bargaining and collecting, analyzing and publishing labor and economic statistics."

Helping the secretary of labor and the many department agencies carry out that mission are a headquarters staff, a deputy secretary, several assistant secretaries, and numerous other officials. Included among the department's agencies are the Administrative Review Board, Benefits Review Board, Bureau of International Labor Affairs, Bureau of Labor Statistics, Employees' Compensation Appeals Board, Employment Standards Administration, Employment and Training Administration, Mine Safety and Health Administration, Occupational Safety and Health Administration, Office of Small Business Programs, Pension and Welfare Benefits Administration, Veterans' Employment and Training Service, and Women's Bureau.

Another agency, the Employment Standards Administration, operates four major program offices: the Office of Federal Contract Compliance Programs, the Office of

Labor-Management Standards, the Office of Workers' Compensation Programs, and the Wage and Hour Division.

Secretary of Housing and Urban Development

In the year 2000 the Secretary of HUD managed 10,000 employees and an annual budget of $32 billion. Headquarters of the department is at 451 Seventh Street, just south of Independence Avenue. The department's stated mission is "a decent, safe, and sanitary home and suitable living environment for every American," attained by "fighting for fair housing, increasing affordable housing and home ownership, reducing homelessness, promoting jobs and economic opportunity, empowering people and communities, [and] restoring the public trust."

HUD works toward this mission with the following agencies: the Office of Housing/Federal Housing Administration, Office of Fair Housing and Equal Opportunity, Office of Public and Indian Housing, Office of Community Planning and Development, Office of Policy Development and Research, Office of Lead Hazard Control, and the Government National Mortgage Association. The acronym GNMA for the last agency was the origin of "Ginnie Mae," the name of a popular kind of home mortgage the agency issues.

Secretary of Health and Human Services

This official managed over 400,000 employees in the year 2000, with an annual budget of $62 billion. "HHS" is located on Independence Avenue over one mile southeast of the White House. The department's mission is "to enhance the health and well-being of Americans by providing for effective health and human services and by fostering strong, sustained advances in the sciences underlying medicine, public health, and social services."

The department is organized into two operating divisions and 12 agencies run by numerous assistant secretaries and other officials. One major operating division,

Experts working for the Centers for Disease Control and Prevention examine a dead pig at a farm in Malaysia as they look for the cause of an encephalitis outbreak in Japan. The CDC, which is one of the many divisions of the Department of Health and Human Services, often travels the globe in attempts to stop the outbreak of disease.

the Public Health Service, includes the following eight agencies: the National Institutes of Health (the government's premier medical research organization), the Food and Drug Administration, the Centers for Disease Control and Prevention, the Agency for Toxic Substances and Disease Registry, the Indian Health Service, the Health Resources and Services Administration, the Substance Abuse and Mental Health Services Administration, and the Agency for Health Care Policy and Research.

The second major operating division, Human Services, includes four agencies: the Program Support Center for the department's own employees, the Administration on Aging, the Administration for Children and Families, and the gigantic Health Care Financing Administration. This last agency, with a $342 billion budget, administers the Medicare and Medicaid programs that provide health care to about one in every four Americans. The Social Security Administration, another huge agency, was once part of the Department of Health and Human Services. But in 1995 the Social Security Administration became an independent agency.

Secretary of Education

Although the cabinet-level Department of Education was established in 1979, a non-cabinet department had bounced around the executive branch since 1867. In 2000 the department had 5,000 employees and an annual budget of $36 billion. Its building on Maryland Avenue is adjacent to the west side of the HHS headquarters. The major goals of the Department of Education are to assure access for all to equal educational opportunity, to help educational institutions improve the quality of education, and to involve the public in federal education programs.

To carry out this mission, the secretary of education, the deputy secretary, and undersecretary have eight agencies running these basic programs: Bilingual Education and Minority Languages Affairs, Civil Rights, Educational Research and Improvement, Elementary and Secondary Education, Postsecondary Education, Special Educational and Rehabilitation Services, Student Financial Assistance Programs, and Vocational and Adult Education.

Secretary of Veterans Affairs

The Department of Veterans Affairs, created in 1988, took over the functions of the former Veterans Administration, which was established in 1930. The department is

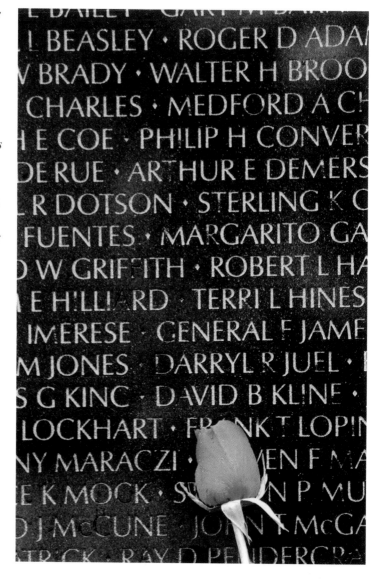

A rose rests against the names of soldiers lost during the conflict in Vietnam engraved on the Vietnam War Memorial. One of the goals of the Department of Veterans Affairs is the creation and upkeep of memorials such as this, which remember those who fought and died for the United States.

located a few hundred yards north of the White House at 810 Vermont Avenue. The stated mission of the department is "to serve America's veterans and their families with dignity and compassion and be their principal advocate in ensuring that they receive medical care, benefits, social support, and lasting memorials promoting the health, welfare and dignity of all veterans in recognition of their service to this Nation."

To do this, the secretary of veterans affairs directed over 200,000 employees in the year 2000 with a budget of $44 billion. Services for veterans and their families include education, insurance, counseling, health care/rehabilitation, pensions, home loans, and burial. Among the numerous active agencies within the Department of Veterans Affairs are: the Veterans Health Administration, VA Research and Development, Veterans Benefits Administration, VA Debt Management Center, the National Cemetery Administration, the Office of Information and Technology, and the Board of Veterans Appeals. Veterans Affairs has regional offices and many smaller offices throughout America.

Secretaries That Shepherd National Resources

Secretary of the Interior

The very old Department of the Interior was established originally to evaluate and protect the nation's land, water, minerals, fish, and wildlife. Through the years the department also constructed irrigation works, enforced mine safety laws, mapped geological surveys, researched minerals, and administered the nation's natural scenic wonders. The scope of the Department of the Interior became immense: over 500 million acres of federal resource lands, about 340 units of the national park system, over 400 wildlife refuges, dozens of fish hatcheries, many historic places, and numerous dams. In addition, the department interacted with Native American reservations and island territories under U.S. administration.

The Department of the Interior headquarters, just one-quarter mile southwest of the White House, was built in 1937. It is considered the first "modern" office building in the nation's capital. No other building in Washington, D.C., at the time had escalators or central air-conditioning.

In the year 2000 the secretary had 76,000 employees with an annual budget of $8 billion. The department's eight divisions include the Bureau of Land Management, the Minerals Management Service, the Office of Surface Mining Reclamation and Enforcement, the Bureau of Reclamation, the U.S. Geological Survey, the U.S. Fish and Wildlife Service, the National Park Service, and the Bureau of Indian Affairs.

Secretary of Agriculture

The headquarters of the Department of Agriculture, begun in 1905, is an enormous complex that straddles Independence Avenue just southeast of the Washington Monument. Almost 100 years later the secretary of agriculture directs 118,000 people with an annual budget of $56 billion. The department's mission is to "enhance the quality of life for the American people by supporting production of agriculture: ensuring a safe, affordable, nutritious, and accessible food supply; caring for agricultural, forest, and range lands; supporting sound development of rural communities; providing economic opportunities for farm and rural residents; expanding global markets for agricultural and forest products and services; and working to reduce hunger in America and throughout the world."

The department has over 20 agencies that operate as seven functional groups: Farm and Foreign Agricultural Services; Food, Nutrition, and Consumer Services; Food Safety; Marketing and Regulatory Programs; Natural Resources and Environment; Research, Education, and Economics; and Rural Development. Among the more vital services provided by the agencies are information dispersal, meat inspection, the Forest Service, and the food stamp program.

Secretary of Commerce

As of this writing, the Department of Commerce's 53,000 employees work with a $6 billion annual budget. The headquarters building is on Constitution Avenue in the nation's capital. The Department of Commerce "promotes job creation, economic growth, sustainable development and improved living standards for all Americans by working in partnership with business, universities, communities and workers." Much of Commerce's function is to promote American businesses abroad, often negotiating international trade agreements. But it also has many domestic duties. The department offers loans and technical assistance to minority-owned businesses. It issues patents, takes the national census, reports weather, and explores oceans and the atmosphere. Also, the National **Telecommunications** and Information Administration is the executive branch's principal voice on all telecommunications and information technology issues.

Secretary of Transportation

The Department of Transportation had an annual budget of $42 billion and 165,000 employees at the dawn of the 21st century. Headquarters of the department is at 400 Seventh Street, SW, south of Independence Avenue and

A U.S. Coast Guard cutter braves stormy seas along the Atlantic coast. The Coast Guard falls under the supervision of the secretary of transportation.

very near the HUD offices. The mission of the department is "to serve the United States by ensuring a fast, safe, efficient, accessible and convenient transportation system that meets our vital national interests and enhances the quality of life of the American people, today and into the future." The secretary of transportation directs 11 operating units. Among these are the Bureau of Transportation Statistics, the U.S. Coast Guard, the Federal Aviation Administration, the Federal Highway Administration, the Federal Railroad Administration, the Federal Transit Administration, the Maritime Administration, and the National Highway Traffic Safety Administration.

Secretary of Energy

The Department of Energy is located in the gigantic Forrestal Building on Independence Avenue, directly east of the Department of Agriculture headquarters. In the year 2000 the secretary of energy supervised 16,000 workers with a $15 billion annual budget. The department has described its short but eventful history: " . . . the Department has shifted its emphasis and focus as the needs of the nation have changed. During the late 1970s, the Department emphasized energy development and regulation. In the 1980s,

A technician checks on a solar reflector in the desert of Arizona. It is one of the many duties of the Department of Energy to oversee the country's use of power and to recommend possible future sources of energy.

nuclear weapons research, development, and production took a priority. Since the end of the Cold War, the Department has focused on environmental clean up of the nuclear weapons complex, nonproliferation and stewardship of the nuclear stockpile, energy efficiency and conservation, and technology transfer and industrial competitiveness." With this rapidly changing focus the department had by 2000 many agencies with varied responsibilities. Agencies for energy resources include Fossil Energy, Nuclear Energy, Energy Efficiency, and Renewable Energy. Later emphasis brought agencies for Defense Programs, Fissile Materials Disposition, Nonproliferation and National Security, Environmental Management, and Radioactive Waste Management.

As the number of officials in the president's cabinet grows, the influence and power of being a cabinet member declines. Although they're still capable of advising the president on key issues, they do not have as much influence as earlier, smaller cabinets.

CHAPTER 6

Past and Future Trends in the Cabinet

CABINET POSTS ARE POSITIONS of great power. But the relative importance of each post advising the president has lessened over the years. In 1790 President Washington was advised by four cabinet officers. In 2000 President William Clinton was advised by 14 cabinet officers. However, this increase in the number of cabinet posts was offset partially by the enormous increase in the size of their departments. In 1790 all the cabinet-level departments together employed less than 1000 workers, including military personnel, and spent less than $100,000. In 2000 all the cabinet-level departments employed over 4 million workers, including military personnel, and spent well over $1 trillion.

Still, the influence of cabinet members with the president has declined. Not only has the number of cabinet officers increased, but over the years other officials have been included in cabinet meetings. The vice president began to regularly attend, as did several others at the president's request. Often sitting in were the ambassador to the United Nations, the director of the Central Intelligence Agency, the chairperson of the economic advisors, director of the Office of Management and Budget and several others, even very influential people on the president's White House staff.

Another development weakened the influence of cabinet members. In 1947 Congress established the National Security Council to advise and assist the president on national security and foreign policies. The council also served as the president's principal arm for coordinating these policies among various government agencies. By law the six council members were the president, vice president, secretary of state, secretary of defense, chairman of the Joint Chiefs of Staff, and the director of Central Intelligence. Thus only two cabinet officers were included. Unstated in the law was the presence of a "national security advisor." This position can be very influential. Under President Nixon, National Security Advisor Henry Kissinger was virtually the number two official in the executive branch for several years.

For those reasons it seemed likely in the 21st century that although cabinet departments would continue to grow in size, the cabinet posts themselves would continue to have less direct influence with the president. In addition it seemed certain that more cabinet-level departments would be added. What were the likely candidates? Among the resource posts, it seemed likely that telecommunications—especially because of the rapidly expanding Internet—will require its own department. By the year 2000 websites numbered in the millions. Worldwide users totaled 200 million. Money from Internet business—called "e-commerce"—was predicted to hit $1 trillion early in the 2000s. America must face several

major issues regarding the Internet. Is security endangered by the Internet? Is pornography too easily available? Should rapidly expanding e-commerce be taxed? A cabinet-level department to wrestle with these issues would seem justified.

Certainly as services from government increase in the future, some aspects may require another cabinet-level department. One very strong candidate is a department to meet the special needs of the elderly. In 2000 about 15 percent of the population was 65 years old or older. In the 21st century that percentage is expected to double. In 2000 the Social Security Administration paid out about $300 billion to 50 million elderly people. The Health Care Financing Administration of the Department of Health and Human Services also paid out enormous amounts to the elderly for Medicare. Financial support of the elderly will

Students use the help of one of their teachers to explore the Internet. Growth in telecommunications may require that a cabinet position be created to manage this rapidly advancing field and to control its influence on our government.

top $1 trillion in the 21st century. These issues will surely require one cabinet-level department.

The number of cabinet-level posts are sure to increase. And the influence of cabinet officers with the president is almost sure to decrease. But cabinet-level departments will continue to grow in size, so cabinet officers will continue to have great power in government.

Glossary

Administration—A group that manages a branch or subdivision of government.

Attorney general—The chief legal advisor of a nation or state.

Civil rights—The rights of personal liberty guaranteed citizens by laws.

Civil servant—A worker in government, usually appointed after a competitive examination.

Commerce—Large-scale buying and selling of products.

Constitution—The laws of a nation that form the basis for determining the power and duties of government and the rights of its citizens.

Executive branch—The branch of government responsible for carrying out ("executing") the affairs of that government.

Federal—The central authority in a form of government that distributes power between a central authority and territorial units or states.

Financial—Relating to the use and distribution of money.

Labor—Word used to include all people working for wages.

Presidency—Relating to the whole term in office of a particular president of the United States.

President *pro tempore* of the Senate—Senator elected by the Senate in the absence of the vice president (who is the "president of the Senate").

Republic—A nation made up of individual states.

Telecommunications—All communication by cable, radio, telegraph, telephone, television, the Internet, and satellite.

Further Reading

Feinberg, Barbara S. *The Cabinet.* New York: Twenty First Century Books, 1995.

Lawson, Don. *Frances Perkins: First Lady of the Cabinet.* New York: Abelard-Schuman, 1966.

Parker, Nancy. *The President's Cabinet and How It Grew.* New York: Parents' Magazine Press, 1978.

Patrick, Diane. *The Executive Branch.* New York: Franklin Watts, 1994.

Richie, Jason. *Secretaries of War, Navy and Defense.* Minneapolis, MN: Oliver Press, 2000.

ABOUT THE AUTHOR: Sam Wellman lives in Kansas. He has degrees from colleges in the Midwest and the Ivy League. He has written a number of biographies of notable people—as diverse as Michelle Kwan, George Washington Carver, Mother Teresa, and Mariah Carey—for both adults and younger readers. He also wrote *The Secretary of State* for the series YOUR GOVERNMENT: HOW IT WORKS.

SENIOR CONSULTING EDITOR Arthur M. Schlesinger, jr. is the leading American historian of our time. He won the Pulitzer Prize for his book *The Age of Jackson* (1945) and again for *A Thousand Days* (1965). This chronicle of the Kennedy Administration also won a National Book Award. Professor Schlesinger is the Albert Schweitzer Professor of the Humanities at the City University of New York, and he has been involved in several other Chelsea House projects, including the REVOLUTIONARY WAR LEADERS and COLONIAL LEADERS series.